SUPER SIMPLE BODY

INSIDE THE EYES

KARIN HALVORSON, M.D.

Consulting Editor, Diane Craig, M.A./Reading Specialist

A Division of ABDO

ABDO
Publishing Company

VISIT US AT WWW.ABDOPUBLISHING.COM

Published by ABDO Publishing Company, a division of
ABDO, P.O. Box 398166, Minneapolis, Minnesota 55439.

Printed in the United States of America,
North Mankato, Minnesota
102012
012013

 PRINTED ON RECYCLED PAPER

Editor: Liz Salzmann
Content Developer: Nancy Tuminelly
Cover and Interior Design: Anders Hanson, Mighty Media
Photo Credits: Shutterstock, Dorling Kindersley RF/Thinkstock,
Colleen Dolphin

Library of Congress Cataloging-in-Publication Data
Halvorson, Karin, 1979-
 Inside the eyes / Karin Halvorson ; consulting editor, Diane Craig.
     p. cm. -- (Super simple body)
 ISBN 978-1-61783-611-4
 1. Eye--Juvenile literature. 2. Vision--Juvenile literature. I. Title.
 QP475.7.H358 2013
 612.8'4--dc23
                          2012028771

Super SandCastle™ books are created by a team of professional
educators, reading specialists, and content developers around five
essential components—phonemic awareness, phonics, vocabulary,
text comprehension, and fluency—to assist young readers as they
develop reading skills and strategies and increase their general
knowledge. All books are written, reviewed, and leveled for guided
reading, early reading intervention, and Accelerated Reader®
programs for use in shared, guided, and independent reading
and writing activities to support a balanced approach to literacy
instruction.

1037782

{ NOTE TO ADULTS }

THIS BOOK is all about encouraging
children to learn the science of how
their bodies work! Be there to help
make science fun and interesting for
young readers. Many activities are
included in this book to help children
further explore what they've learned.
Some require adult assistance and/
or permission. Make sure children have
appropriate places where they can do
the activities safely.

Children may also have questions about
what they've learned. Offer help and
guidance when they have questions.
Most of all encourage them to keep
exploring and learning new things!

CONTENTS

YOUR BODY

YOUR EYES

You're amazing! So is your body!

Your body has a lot of different parts. Your eyes, ears, brain, stomach, lungs, and heart all work together every day. They keep you moving. Even when you don't realize it.

Eyes are amazing! From when you wake up until you sleep, they help you out. They are there when you pick out your favorite shirt, read a book, or catch a ball.

CAN YOU THINK OF OTHER WAYS THAT YOU USE YOUR EYES?

ALL ABOUT THE
EYE

Your eyes are your windows to the world. They let you see.

But you can only see part of them when you look in the mirror. What goes on *inside* your eye?

SOFT ON THE INSIDE

Eyes are round balls filled with a special jelly. It's called vitreous humor (**VI-TREE-UHS HYOO-MUR**). It keeps your eyes round.

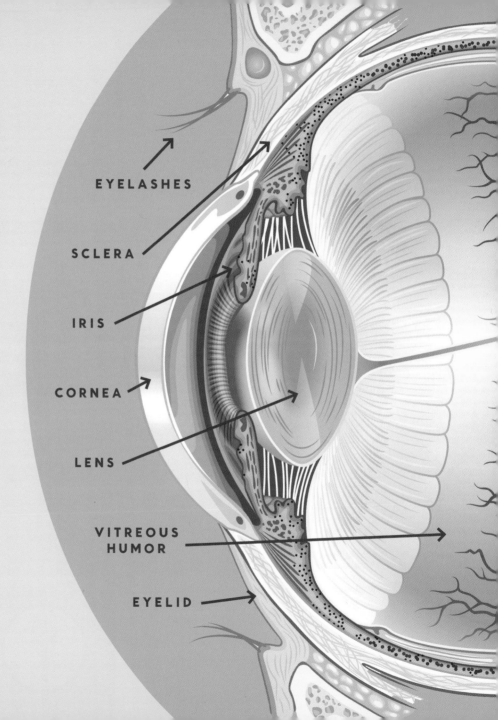

EYELASHES

SCLERA

IRIS

CORNEA

LENS

VITREOUS HUMOR

EYELID

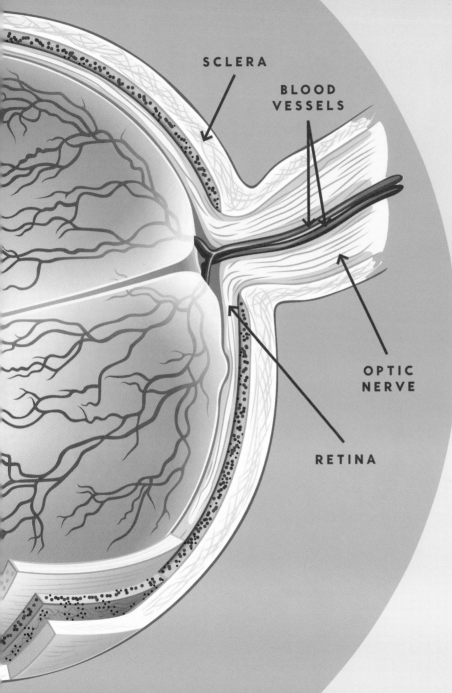

SCLERA

BLOOD VESSELS

OPTIC NERVE

RETINA

TOUGH ON THE OUTSIDE

The outsides of your eyes are made of strong **tissues**. They surround the jelly. This outside area is the sclera (SKLER-UH). It is the white part of your eyes.

IT TAKES TWO!

Eyes are so great that your body has two! Your eyes work together to tell if something is far away or up close. You can see nearby objects and far away objects at the same time. That's because you have two eyes.

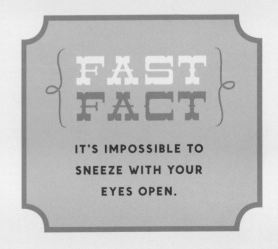

FAST FACT

IT'S IMPOSSIBLE TO SNEEZE WITH YOUR EYES OPEN.

SOCKET TO ME!

Your eyes are important. So important you have an army to protect them.

EYE SOCKETS

The first guard in your army is your **skull**. It has **sockets** that your eyes sit in. If you place your hands flat over your eyes, you feel the bones, not your eyes. This keeps large objects from hitting your eyes.

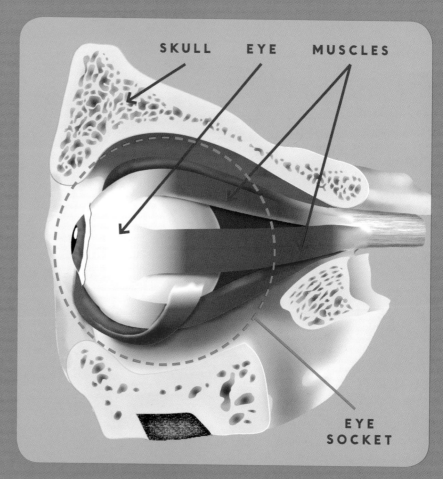

SKULL   EYE   MUSCLES

EYE SOCKET

THE EYE SITS INSIDE THE EYE SOCKET

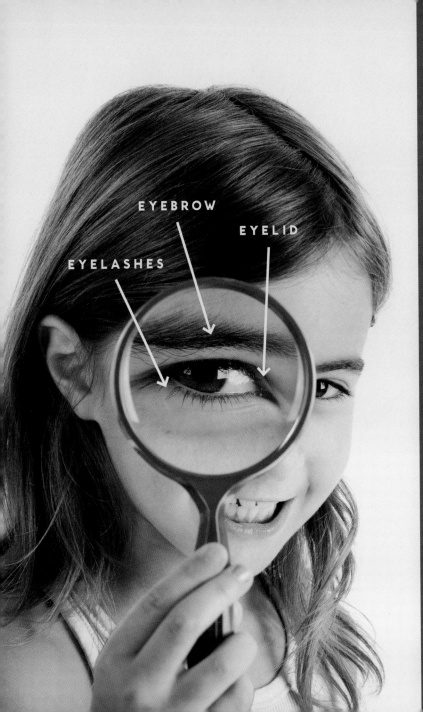

EYELASHES

EYEBROW

EYELID

EYEBROWS

Your eyebrows are lines of hair right above your eyes. They stop sweat from getting into your eyes.

EYELIDS & EYELASHES

Your eyelids also guard your eyes. Your eyelids have hairs on them called eyelashes. They keep small things such as dust and bugs out of your eyes.

THINK & BLINK

You blink about once every 5 seconds. That's more than 15,000 times a day!

KEEP IT CLEAN

You blink to keep bugs and dust out of your eyes. But did you know that blinking also cleans your eyes? Right next to each eyeball is a special **gland** that makes tears. On the other side of each eye is a tear duct.

When you blink, tears squirt onto your eyes. Your eyelids spread the tears over your eyeballs. The tears pick up any dirt and dust in your eyes. Then the tears flow into your tear ducts, taking the dirt away.

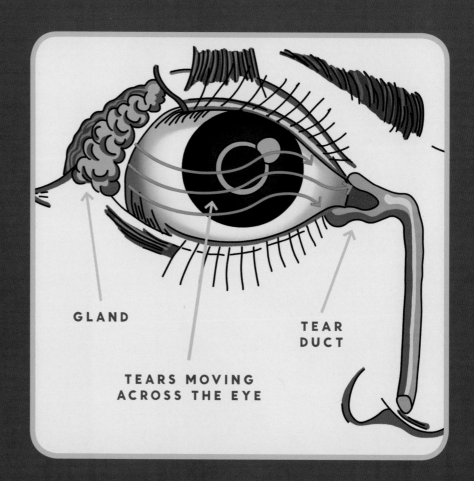

GLAND

TEARS MOVING
ACROSS THE EYE

TEAR
DUCT

When you cry, you make a lot of tears. Your tear ducts can't drain all the tears away. They have nowhere else to go, so they run down your face!

CAN YOU THINK OF OTHER REASONS THAT PEOPLE MAKE TEARS?

FAST FOCUS

IMPROVE YOUR FOCUS!

WHAT YOU NEED: OPEN SPACE, A FRIEND, STOPWATCH, TENNIS BALL, BASEBALL, SOCCER BALL, BASKETBALL

HOW TO DO IT

1. Sit with your eyes closed. Have your friend put each ball a different distance away from you.

2. Open your eyes when your friend starts the stopwatch. Look for the balls.

3. Name the balls from largest to smallest as fast as you can. Have your friend time you. Then switch and time your friend. Who can do it faster?

4. Try it again with the balls in different spots. Or use smaller objects to make it harder. Keep improving your time!

WHAT'S HAPPENING?

This activity helps you see and recognize things quickly. This can help you protect your eyes. You'll be able to see something coming at your eyes in time to close them or duck out of the way.

LIGHT THE WAY

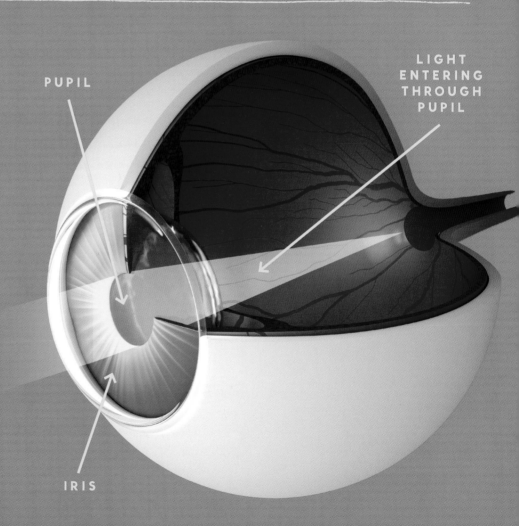

Light is important in order to see. The darker it is, the harder it is to see. If there is no light, you can't see at all.

THE PUPILS

Your pupils (PYOO-PUHLZ) are the black circles in the middle of each eye. They look solid, but they are actually holes! Light enters your eyes through your pupils.

PUPIL

LIGHT ENTERING THROUGH PUPIL

IRIS

THE IRISES

The colored parts of your eyes are called the irises (EYE-RIS-EZ). The irises are special muscles. They make your pupils bigger or smaller. That controls the amount of light that comes into your eyes.

When there is a lot of light, your pupil gets smaller. It lets in only as much light as you need.

When there is little light, your pupil gets bigger. It's trying to let in as much light as possible.

SEE CHANGE

MAKE YOUR PUPILS GROW!

WHAT YOU NEED: PAPER, MARKER, CRAFT FOAM, SCISSORS, LARGE SEWING NEEDLE, ELASTIC, MIRROR

HOW TO DO IT

1. Draw the shape of an eye patch on a piece of paper. Cut it out. Trace the shape on a piece of craft foam. Cut out the foam shape.

2. Use a large needle to make two holes at the top of the eye patch.

3. Thread the elastic through both holes. Hold the eye patch up to your eye. Tie the ends of the elastic together so it fits around your head.

4. Look at both of your pupils in the mirror. They should be about the same size. Use the eye patch to cover one eye for 15 minutes. Take the eye patch off and look in the mirror again. Are your pupils still the same size?

WHAT'S HAPPENING?

When you see, light enters both of your eyes. They work together. If one eye isn't taking in any light, then the other eye needs to take in more. So its pupil gets bigger.

THE COLOR OF LIGHT

A RAINBOW IN A BUBBLE

WHAT YOU NEED: 1 CUP WATER, 4 TABLESPOONS DISHWASHING LIQUID, 2 TABLESPOONS GLYCERIN, LARGE BOWL, SPOON, CHENILLE STEMS, COOKIE CUTTER

HOW TO DO IT

1. Put the water, dishwashing liquid, and glycerin in a bowl. Mix it with a spoon.

2. Wrap a chenille stem around the cookie cutter. Press it against the cookie cutter all the way around.

3. When you've gone all the way around, twist the ends of the stem together. Slide the stem off of the cookie cutter. Twist the ends onto another chenille stem to make a handle for your bubble wand.

4. Dip the wand in the soap mixture. Blow bubbles. Watch them closely. What color are they? Do you see more than one color?

WHAT'S HAPPENING?

The light from the sun and most lightbulbs is called white light. But it is really made up of every color except black. When white light hits a soapy bubble, the colors in the light separate so you can see them.

GET FOCUSED!

Light enters your eyes through your pupils. There is a lens (LENZ) behind each pupil that focuses the light. This lets you see things clearly.

The lenses focus by changing shape. To see something far away, the lenses get tall and thin. To see something close up, they get short and fat.

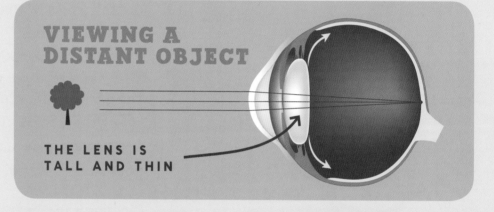

VIEWING A DISTANT OBJECT

THE LENS IS TALL AND THIN

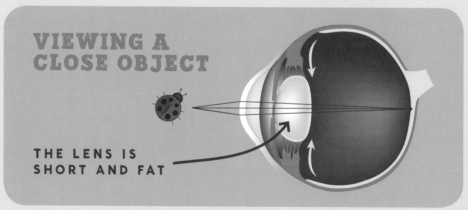

VIEWING A CLOSE OBJECT

THE LENS IS SHORT AND FAT

There are many different kinds of lenses. Some flip images, others make images larger or smaller.

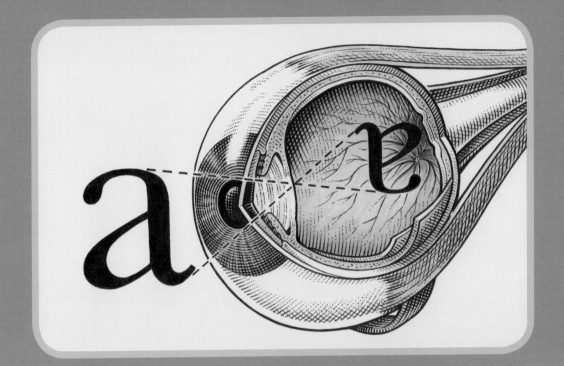

A raindrop on a window is a great example of a lens. Next time you're by a rainy window, check one out! If you look close enough, everything on the other side will be upside down!

EYE SPY

MAKE A LIQUID LENS

WHAT YOU NEED: PAPER, MARKER, PLASTIC WRAP, TAPE, WATER, TEASPOON

HOW TO DO IT

1. Write your favorite word on a piece of paper in different sizes. Cover the words with plastic wrap. Tape it down.

2. Use the teaspoon to put a small drop of water on the plastic wrap.

3. The drop of water acts like a lens, like the lenses in your eyes.

4. What happens to the words underneath? Do they look larger? Try using bigger or smaller drops. See what happens when you play with them!

WHAT'S HAPPENING?

The smaller water drops are rounder on top, so they make things look bigger. The larger water drops are flatter on top. This means they don't change the size of the words as much.

RODS & CONES

After light passes through the pupils and lenses, it hits the backs of your eyes. Inside the back of each eye is a retina (RE-TE-NUH). The retinas have special cells called rods and cones. The rods and cones **react** to the light that comes into your eyes.

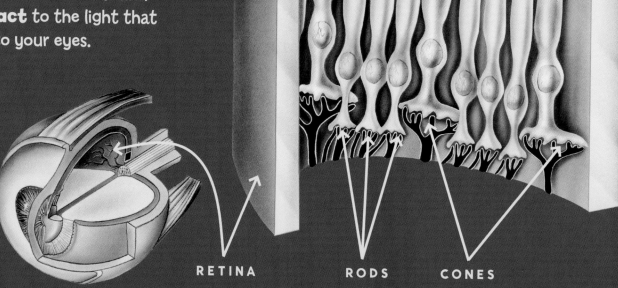

RETINA   RODS   CONES

24

Rods sense shapes. They help you see when there is only a little light.

Cones sense color. They work better with a lot of light. That's why things don't look as colorful at night.

DAY

NIGHT

SEEING STARS

FUN WITH AFTERIMAGES

WHAT YOU NEED: COLORED CRAFT PAPER, WHITE PAPER, BLACK MARKER, STOPWATCH OR CLOCK WITH SECOND HAND

26

HOW TO DO IT

1. Cut a star out of blue paper. Glue it to a red sheet of paper.

2. Draw a small black dot in the center of the star. Lay a white piece of paper next to the star. Put a black dot in the center of the white paper.

3. Stare at the black dot on the star for 30 seconds. Then move your eyes to the dot on the white paper. What do you see?

4. Try it with different colors. See what happens!

WHAT'S HAPPENING?

What you see on the white paper is an afterimage. The color changes because the cones in your eyes get tired. The color of the afterimage is the complementary color of the original.

SPIN CYCLE

MIXING COLORED LIGHT

WHAT YOU NEED: PAPER PLATE, RULER, SCISSORS, MARKERS, TAPE, SHARPENED PENCIL

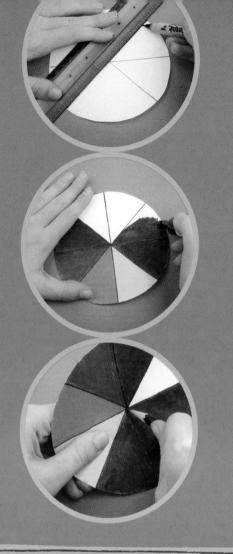

HOW TO DO IT

1. Cut out the center of the paper plate.

2. Use the ruler to divide the circle into eight equal sections. Make sure every line goes through the middle of the circle.

3. Use a marker to make each section a different color. Use red, blue, yellow, purple, green, brown, and orange. Leave one section white.

4. Make a small hole in the center of the plate. Put the pencil through it with the eraser on the colored side. Tape it in place.

5. Spin it on the pencil tip like a top. What colors do you see? What happens when you make tops with different colors?

WHAT'S HAPPENING?

When colors of light mix together they make white! When the top is still, you can see all the colors. When it spins, the top will look white or gray.

EYE
CAN DO IT!
YOU CAN TOO!

MAKE A MODEL OF YOUR EYE!

WHAT YOU NEED: EGG CARTON, PENCIL, WHITE BALLOON, WATER, WHITE CIRCLE STICKER, MARKERS

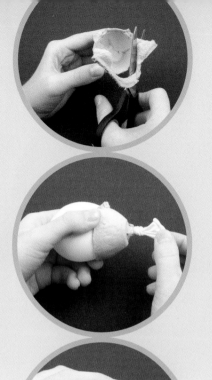

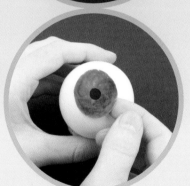

HOW TO DO IT

1 Cut out a single eggcup from the egg carton. Use a pencil to poke a hole in the bottom.

2 Put water in the white balloon. Fill it until it's a little smaller than the eggcup. Tie it closed. Put the balloon in the eggcup. Pull the knot through the hole. The knot of the balloon is the **optic nerve**.

3 Draw a small black circle in the middle of the sticker. Color the rest of the sticker the color of your iris. Stick it on the top of the balloon. Now you have a model of your eye.

WHAT'S HAPPENING?

How many parts of your eyes can you name? Look back in the book if you need help!

GLAND - an organ in the body that makes chemicals that your body needs.

NERVE - one of the threads in the body that take messages to and from the brain.

OPTIC - having to do with the eye or vision.

REACT - to do something in response to something learned or sensed.

SKULL - the bones that protect the brain and form the face and head.

SOCKET - an opening that holds something.

TISSUE - a group of similar cells that forms one part of a plant or animal.

GLOSSARY